T0353842

AuthorHouse™ UK
1663 Liberty Drive
Bloomington, IN 47403 USA
www.authorhouse.co.uk
UK TFN: 0800 0148641 (Toll Free inside the UK)
UK Local: 02036 956322 (+44 20 3695 6322 from outside the UK)

Because of the dynamic nature of the Internet, any web addresses or links contained in this book may have changed
since publication and may no longer be valid. The views expressed in this work are solely those of the author and do
not necessarily reflect the views of the publisher, and the publisher hereby disclaims any responsibility for them.

@ Illustration Katri Hansson

Any people depicted in stock imagery provided by Getty Images are models,
and such images are being used for illustrative purposes only.
Certain stock imagery © Getty Images.

This book is printed on acid-free paper.

ISBN: 979-8-8230-8882-4 (sc)
ISBN: 979-8-8230-8884-8 (hc)
ISBN: 979-8-8230-8883-1 (e)

Library of Congress Control Number: 2024915137

Print information available on the last page.

Published by AuthorHouse 07/23/2024

authorHOUSE

BRAKE!

Catarina Hansson | Katri Hansson

My Grandma is my best friend even though she is almost 100 years old. One day she got it into her head that she wanted to try out my new roller skates.

I try to tell Grandma that roller skates are not a good idea because she lives by a dirt road out in the country. Her garden is all grass and flower beds and there are things everywhere. Grandma just giggles and rolls her eyes. She wants to try them right now.

– "Okay, but then you'll have to put on protection," I say, holding out my index finger as firmly as Mum usually does.

– "Protection? Do I really need protection?" Grandma asks a little sourly.

– "You have to have protection if you're going roller skating," I say firmly.

– "I think I've got something I can use in the attic," says Grandma and quickly climbs up the ladder with her skirt fluttering around her legs.

She's rummaging around in the attic, so the dust is swirling down through the open attic hatch.

I'm sitting in the kitchen trying to figure out how to get my grandmother to forget about the roller skates, but I can't think of anything. Once my grandmother has made up her mind, it usually turns out the way she wants. And I just wanted to cosy up with freshly baked cinnamon buns and lemonade out in the garden.

– "Come and see what I've found," Grandma calls.

Curious, I climb up the ladder and peer into the attic.

Grandma rummages around in a big chest, so old hats and shoes are scattered about. An old soldier's helmet fits perfectly on her head. Grandad's worn gardening gloves protect her hands. Grandma ties long rag socks around her elbows and scarves around her knees. Finally, she ties a large, red-striped pillow to protect her bottom.

I'm so nervous about my grandma leaving that I have to go to the outhouse. There I sit and look out through the mosquito net in the door and listen to Grandma's happy screams and laughter, the cackling of the hens and the dog Roll barking and barking.

I hardly dare to think of all the things that could happen. What if Grandma falls? Or drives straight into the outhouse?

My heart beats hard when I hear the gravel rattling and my grandmother comes round the corner of the house at great speed.

Grandma rides over the grass and flower beds so that the flowers swirl around. Just then, Grandma comes running past the outhouse with a panicked hen that has landed on top of the old helmet. Terrified, the rooster flies up onto the porch and wakes up the pig, who is sunbathing peacefully.

The pig runs away grunting across the grass, scaring both the goose and the other hens. I stay in the loo, too scared to go out.

I should be used to it because strange things always happen at my grandmother's. If she's not climbing trees, she's building a tree house or painting the outhouse green and pink.

She never tells me I can't do things. However, I often have to tell my grandmother.

11

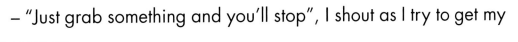

– "Help!" screams Grandma. "Where is the brake?"

– "Just grab something and you'll stop", I shout as I try to get my trousers up.

No sooner said than done, Grandma grabs the first, best thing she passes.

Grandma grabs hold of Bella the cow's tail. Bella shouts and runs away across the meadow.

I press my nose against the mosquito net and watch Grandma disappear across the meadow, hanging by Bella's tail.

– "Grandma!" I cry out in despair, my heart in my throat.

I rush out and run after them as fast as I can. My heart is beating so hard I can hardly breathe. They disappear into the forest with a crash. I think it's probably the last time I see both Bella and Grandma.

But then suddenly I find them! Bella is standing a little way into the forest, looking sour. She looks at me, moos, and slowly starts to walk back to the meadow while wagging her sore tail.

Grandma is sitting in the middle of a large anthill. Her hair spreads under her helmet, which has slipped aside. The hen is standing on the helmet with an angry look.

   – "Good thing I tied a pillow to the back," Grandma sighs and gets up from the anthill.

– "I think I'm going to train Bella to drag me to the village," says Grandma and laughs. "Then it will be quick to shop".

– "You'd better ask Bella if she wants to go first," I sigh.

My legs are still a bit shaky.

– "I'm sure she does. What cow doesn't want to run to the village?"

– "Cock-a-doodle-doo," says the hen on top of the helmet, laying an egg in sheer terror. The egg lands in the soft moss.

– "But you'll have to stay at home, my little hen," says Grandma. "What would it look like if I went round with a chicken on my head? People might think I'm crazy."

Grandma takes the chicken under her arm and starts walking home. It doesn't go very fast because she has forgotten to take off her roller skates.

– "I'm going to buy my own pair of roller skates, so we can go skating together," says Grandma happily. "You are my best friend."

A warm and cosy feeling spreads in my stomach. And suddenly nothing feels difficult anymore, because Grandma is actually my best friend too.

As we walk past Bella, the cow stares at Grandma and lowers her horns. She's not going to play any more today, that's for sure.

– "I can't believe you found us even though we went as fast as a rocket," says Grandma, smiling." How lucky you are to be so wise."

I nod, what would Grandma do without me?

– "Grandma, maybe you should take off your roller skates?" I say gently. "You'll probably walk better then."

– "No, nonsense! I know how to do this now, you can see that," Grandma says and stumbles on.

Tomorrow I'm going to show Grandma my new skateboard.

Printed in the United States
by Baker & Taylor Publisher Services